# THIS BOOK BELONGS TO:

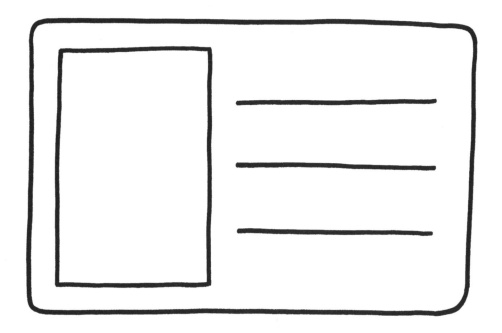

# SURPRISE yourself

## Get Out of Your Head and Into the World

### LISA CURRIE

A TarcherPerigee Book

tarcherperigee

An imprint of Penguin Random House LLC
New York, New York 10019

Proprietary ISBN 9781101949054

Printed in the United States of America

1   3   5   7   9   10   8   6   4   2

Book design by Lisa Currie

DEDICATED TO MY FUTURE SELF:

Please remember to spend less time trying to predict
what "could" happen in every scenario & more time
just showing up to see what does happen.
It's more fun that way.

PS— I like that new thing you've done with your hair.

# welcome!

This book is both an adventure guide and a comfort blanket. Some pages will nudge you into new scenarios and creative escapades! Other pages will remind you to be kind to yourself and give you ideas to recoup when you need to.

Some pages are quickies to complete in an hour or less: other pages can fill up a whole day! And a few pages are made to be carried with you throughout the week— to go about your normal routine with fresh eyes and a playful mission.

## IS THIS A SOLO ADVENTURE OR A TEAM SPORT?

Both! All the pages in this book are either A) a fun way to connect with another person, or B) a fun way to connect with your own sweet self and the world around you. Choose whatever you're in the mood for.

## WHERE TO BEGIN?

Begin anywhere! Don't mull it over too much. This book is about DOING. Just flip to a random page and start there.

Some prompts will attract you right away and feel easy. Others might give you a twinge of nerves or uncertainty. Pay attention to those feelings. Is that page calling to you from just outside your comfort zone? Is it inviting you to explore a part of yourself (or the world) that feels too silly, too vulnerable? Go there. Have some fun! You might surprise yourself.

xox lisa

PS— In the back of this book you'll find a checklist of all the pages to color in as you do them. Cut out the three checklists and stick them somewhere handy— like on a bedroom wall, the fridge, or your bathroom mirror. Celebrate your progress!

let's begin!

# FOLLOW THIS MAP
## AS BEST YOU CAN

Begin on the sidewalk outside your house or apartment building & fill in the blanks as you go. Wander slowly, noticing the sky, the ground, the landscape, the buildings, the people, the front yards, the smells, the sounds! When you get home, decorate the map with even more details. Everything you can remember.

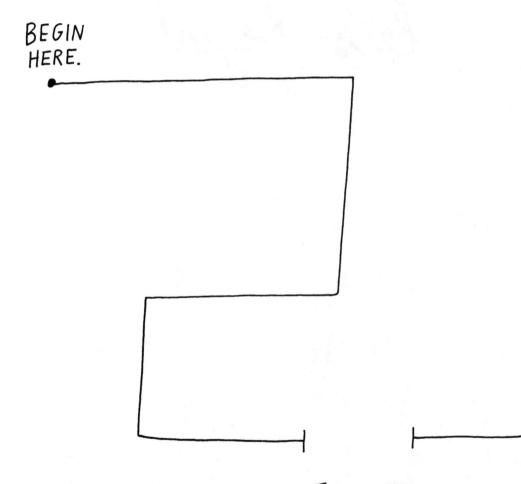

BEGIN
HERE.

JUMP OVER
THIS OBSTACLE.
WHAT WAS IT?

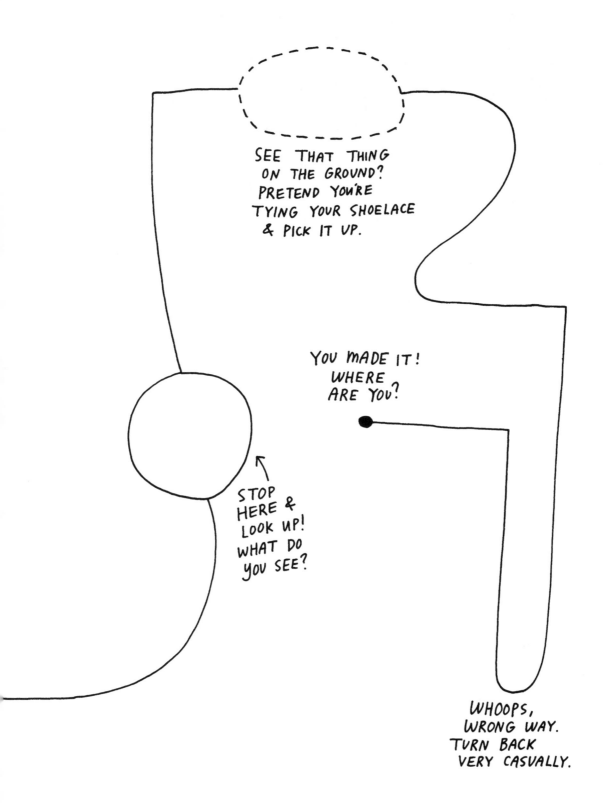

# FIND YOURSELF A
# GOOD-LUCK CHARM

While you're out in the world today, be on the lookout for a small token that fits into your pocket and feels lucky to you. It might be a gold coin found on the sidewalk, a novelty key ring that reminds you of home, or a smooth pebble that feels calming in your hand. Doodle your new good-luck charm here.

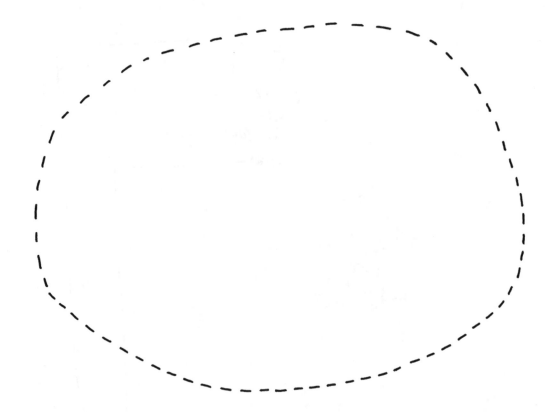

Describe the kind of luck you hope it will bring.

# GO BAREFOOT

At home or around your neighborhood today, try to find all four of these surfaces to wiggle your toes in. Take a few minutes to enjoy the sensation!

### SOFT/SQUISHY

LOCATION:

### CRUNCHY

LOCATION:

### WET

LOCATION:

### WARM

LOCATION:

# ADOPT A new HOUSEPLANT

I SHALL NAME YOU:

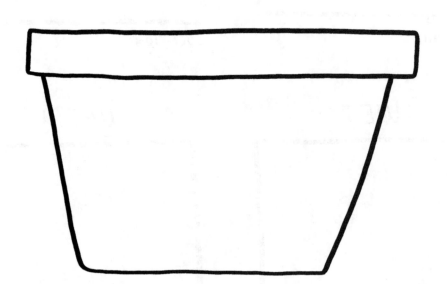

## PERSONALITY TRAITS

\* Prefers to hang out in the shade / sunshine (circle one).

\* Needs a drink of $H_2O$ every _____ days.

\* Its favorite genre of music seems to be _____.

# STEAL SOMEONE ELSE'S MORNING ROUTINE

Who will you choose: a friend you admire? a personal hero? Explain why you chose this person & what magic you hope their morning routine will bring you.

THEIR MORNING ROUTINE (Ask them or look it up online.)

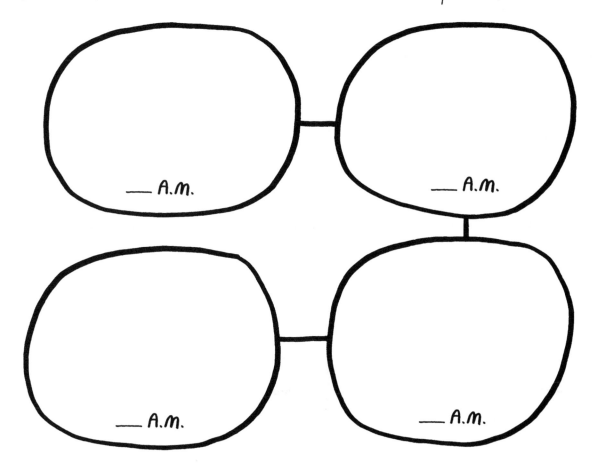

__ A.M.

__ A.M.

__ A.M.

__ A.M.

Try it yourself tomorrow morning, or every morning this week if you can!

# CELEBRATE A FRIENDIVERSARY

Organize to celebrate an upcoming friendiversary, or even a belated one!

| FRIEND'S NAME | DATE WE MET OR BECAME FRIENDS | IDEA FOR HOW TO CELEBRATE OUR FRIENDIVERSARY! Something nostaligic? silly? sweet? |
|---|---|---|
| | | |
| | | |
| | | |
| | | |

# MAKE YOURSELF
# A JAR OF COMPLIMENTS

nice THINGS
PEOPLE HAVE
SAID ABOUT me
✱ Grab one as needed!

Brainstorm all the nicest things you've been told about yourself onto scraps of paper, then drop them into a glass jar. Whenever you're given a compliment that makes you feel good about yourself (no matter how small!) drop it in the jar, too. Grab one whenever you need a nudge of self-confidence or some good vibes!

# ASK YOUR GRANDMA
## FOR A RECIPE
### (OR SOMEONE ELSE'S GRANDMA)

INGREDIENTS—

METHOD—

& cook it for dinner or dessert this week!

# SCREW GENDER ROLES!

SOME GENDER STEREOTYPES THAT FRUSTRATE ME:

girls CAN'T _____.

boys SHOULDN'T _____.

women AREN'T _____.

men DON'T _____.

This weekend, do something that celebrates who you are and what you're curious about, without paying any mind to gender norms (how men & women "should" look or act). Try something new, or pick up an old hobby! Jot down some ideas below.

# INVENT YOUR OWN
# YOGA MOVES
## (NO EXPERIENCE NEEDED!)

Think of three slow, simple stretches that feel good on your body. You might fold forward at the hips, do some gentle neck rolls, lie on the floor & hug your legs. Give each new move a silly name, to help remember them! Practice your moves every day this week, each for a minute or two.

① THE _____

_____

What does it look like?

② THE _____

What does it look like?

③ THE _____

What does it look like?

# MAKE A PROMISE
## TO YOURSELF

From now on I will try to _____

_____

even if _____.

This is important to me because

_____

_____.

How I will keep this promise:

_____

_____

Signed: _____     date: _____

# ORGANIZE A CARE PACKAGE FOR SOMEONE

for: _____

to say:  
☐ I LOVE YOU!  
☐ THANK YOU SO MUCH  
☐ (JUST BECAUSE)  
☐ I HOPE YOU'RE OKAY ♡  
☐ _____

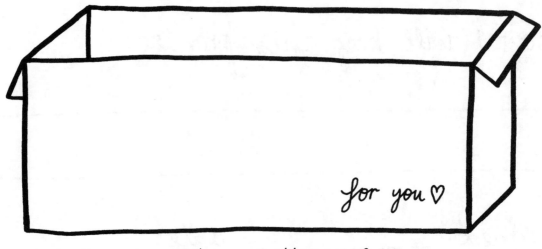

for you ♡

What are you putting inside?

# GO STARGAZING

Find a place to watch the sky tonight. Roll out a blanket on the grass (or beach, if you can!) & get acquainted with this beautiful universe we call home.

## SHOOTING STAR TALLY
### (make a wish!)

## HOW FULL IS THE MOON TONIGHT?

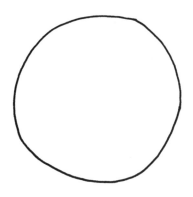

## STARGAZING PLAYLIST

1.

2.

3.

4.

5.

15

# DIP A TOE OUTSIDE
# YOUR COMFORT ZONE

What are some things you're curious to try, but they happen to be just outside (or way outside) your current comfort zone? Pick one to try this week.

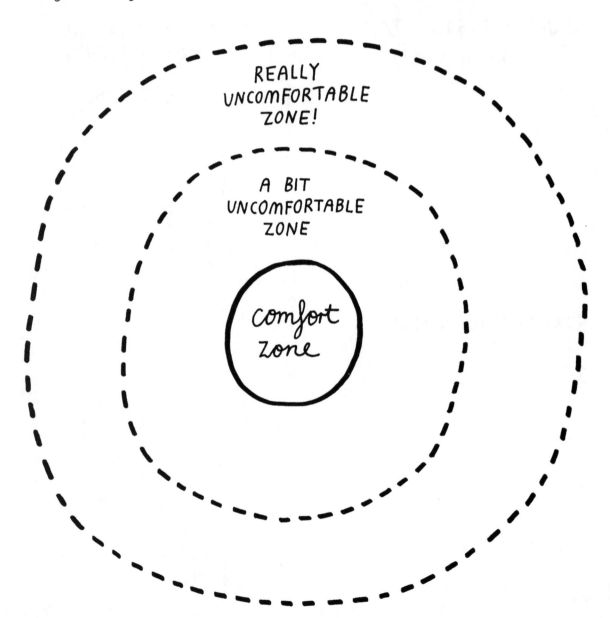

REALLY
UNCOMFORTABLE
ZONE!

A BIT
UNCOMFORTABLE
ZONE

comfort
zone

# NOSE BINGO

This game is best played while wandering around a city, or at the mall. Sniff out as many of these scents as you can & write a quick description of each one. If you want to play with a friend, three in a row wins!

| | | |
|---|---|---|
| A SMELL THAT REMINDS ME OF HOME | THE SCENT OF AN EX-LOVER'S PERFUME OR AFTERSHAVE | A SMELL I RECOGNIZE BEFORE I SEE WHERE IT'S COMING FROM |
| A SMELL THAT CONFUSES ME | BONUS SMELL! | A SMELL THAT REMINDS ME OF A VACATION I'VE BEEN ON |
| ONE OF MY FAVORITE SMELLS EVER! | A SCENT THAT REMINDS ME OF MY GRANDPARENTS | THE SCENT OF MY YOUTH! |

# GO WINDOW-SHOPPING AT AN ART GALLERY

Visit the largest art gallery (or history museum) in your city and, as you wander around, mull over which of these priceless artworks you'll be taking home today. This one's cute, is it too big for the guest bathroom? What about that one, that'd be nice for mom's birthday! Use these pages to sketch a wish list of all your favorite pieces of art & what you plan to do with them.

The painting you'll wrap up for your best friend on their next birthday.

The perfect artwork to hang in your bedroom.

Decide on a small sculpture to sit atop this plinth. Where in your house will it live?

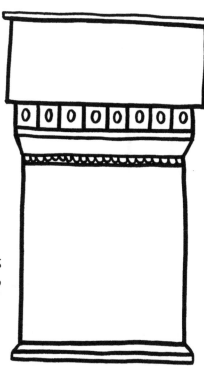

19

# STAY HOME INSTEAD

## RSVP

YOU'VE BEEN INVITED TO:

_____

☐ NO, THANKS! I'LL BE
STAYING HOME TO DO
THIS INSTEAD:

LOVE FROM _____ X

# LEARN ABOUT SOMEONE ELSE'S RELIGION

Have a chat with someone who has a different spiritual practice than you do, especially one you don't know much about. Listen with curiosity & an open mind.

The religion they practice is: _____

WHAT IS ONE OF THE BEST LESSONS YOUR RELIGION HAS TAUGHT YOU?

THOUGHTS ON THE AFTERLIFE?

IN WHAT WAYS DO YOU WORSHIP?

WHAT DO YOU THINK IS A COMMON MISCONCEPTION ABOUT YOUR FAITH?

# SHARE YOUR VULNERABILITY WITH A FRIEND

Ask each other the questions below and create a mind map together. Use the same pen so it becomes a mishmash of your thoughts collectively. Your answers might not be the same, but you're in this together!

Have a cup of tea in your hands, or a glass of wine. Listen to each other gently, without judgment or rush.

WHAT DO YOU SPEND MOST OF YOUR TIME WORRYING ABOUT?

IN WHAT WAYS DO YOU FEEL SELF-CONSCIOUS ABOUT YOUR BODY?

WHAT ARE YOU SCARED OF WHEN YOU GO OUT INTO THE WORLD?

IN WHAT WAYS DO YOU FEEL YOU'RE NOT ENOUGH?

IN WHAT WAYS DO YOU FEEL YOU'RE TOO MUCH?

# FIX SOMETHING
## THAT'S BEEN BUGGING YOU

| BEFORE | AFTER |
|--------|-------|
|        |       |

# MAKE A VIDEO TIME CAPSULE OF THE PEOPLE YOU LOVE

## WHO WILL YOU COLLECT FOOTAGE OF?

Who are the special people in your life? Use your camera phone to record.

## WHAT MOMENTS WILL YOU CAPTURE?

The ordinary moments often end up being the most special to us. Those tiny details that make a person who they are, that define why we love them so much.

CAR KARAOKE TO THEIR FAVORITE SONG

THE WAY THEY LAUGH

# THE COLOR OF THE DAY
# IS YELLOW

As you go about your business today allow yourself to notice the color YELLOW everywhere. Choose something YELLOW when you get dressed today. Be attracted to the color YELLOW in what you buy, which shops you walk into, the books you pick up, what you eat for lunch, and who you smile at on the sidewalk.

## MY PERSONAL INVENTORY
## OF yellow things*

*Clothing, books, artwork & other YELLOW things you own.

Follow the color YELLOW today! Where does it lead you?
map out all the YELLOW in your day.

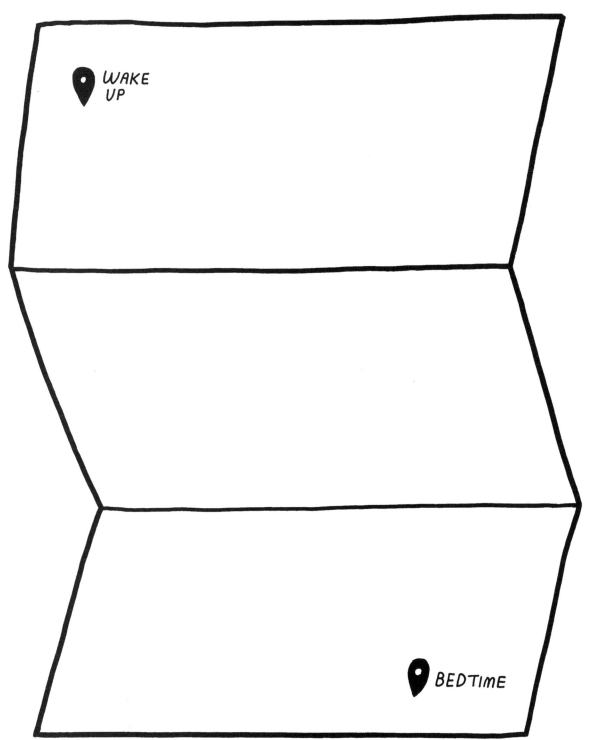

# TAKE THE FIRST STEP

Think of an idea or project that's been knocking around in your brain for the longest time. Something you want to bring to life but you haven't gotten around to it yet. Maybe even, it intimidates you a little. Think of what the first step could be. It doesn't need to be a perfect plan, just a place to begin. Set aside at least two hours this week to work on it.

THE FIRST STEP:
what is it?
↓

# HUNT FOR EMOJI IN THEIR NATURAL HABITAT

Re-create or find these 12 emoji in the world around you. Some you'll spot right away; some you'll need to be a bit more resourceful & creative in bringing them to life. Take a photo to document each one you find. Ask a friend to join you!

Give yourself a time limit to find as many as you can. Say, two hours, or a day!

# A SMALL ACT OF TRIBUTE

What was the last movie or documentary to inspire you, delight you, or leave you in awe? This weekend do something in a small act of tribute to that film and how much it meant to you personally.

THE MOVIE:

I WAS INSPIRED BY:

MY SMALL ACT OF TRIBUTE:

An example:

THE MOVIE: Frances Ha.

I WAS INSPIRED BY: The main character, Frances, her charming clumsiness in life & how she was stubborn in her dreams of being a dancer but also learned when to compromise for her own happiness.

MY SMALL ACT OF TRIBUTE: Take my first dance class this weekend—even though I'm nervous!

# ORDER SOMETHING ELSE

MY REGULAR ORDER

SOMETHING NEW TO TRY

# LEAVE A BOOK BEHIND
# FOR A STRANGER

(ON A PARK BENCH, ON THE TRAIN, AT A CAFÉ)

Write an inscription on the inside cover. Explain what you liked about the book & why you've decided to pass it on to someone else.

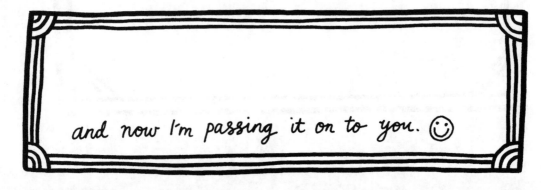

and now I'm passing it on to you. ☺

# HAVE SOMEONE SIT FOR YOU WHILE YOU DRAW THEIR PORTRAIT

## MY MODEL & MUSE

How should they pose? A prop in their hands? A certain facial expression?

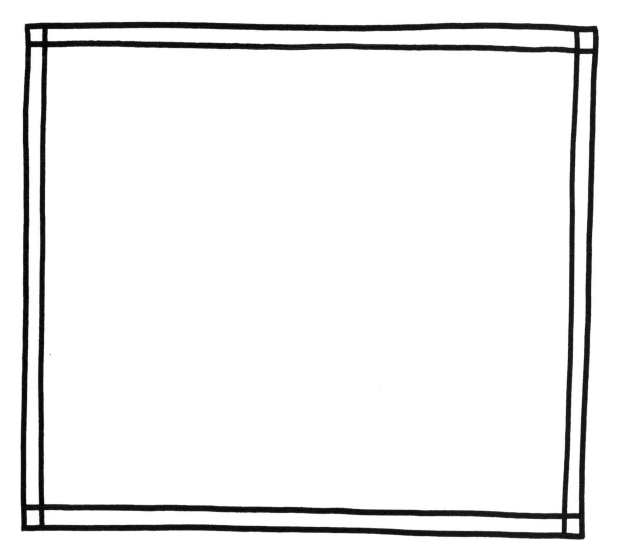

Give the portrait to your lovely model when you're done. Don't forget to sign your name & date the work of art. Maybe scribble a kind message, too!

# A WEEK OF "YES"

This week pay attention to all the opportunities and invitations that come into your daily life. They might be small, like a welcoming smile from a passing neighbor ready for a chat, or they might be bigger, like an invitation to an event.

This week, say YES to some things you would normally turn away from. Follow your curiosity into the unknown! See where you end up!

## A FEW THINGS I SAID YES TO THIS WEEK:

# DOODLE YOUR WAY
# THROUGH THE ALPHABET

The perfect place to do this is if you commute on the bus or train, or any waiting room you happen to be stuck in. The gist is: doodle one thing for every letter of the alphabet, but only things you can see in the room you're in right now, or out the window. Ready? And go.

I SPY SOMETHING BEGINNING WITH...

F

G

H

I

J

K

L

m

N

O

P

Q

R

S

T U

V

W

X

Y

Z

# COMPLETE A JIGSAW PUZZLE

\# OF PIECES: _____

MY ASSISTANT:

_____

(or: ☐ don't need one)

DESIGN ON THE BOX

## PROGRESS REPORT

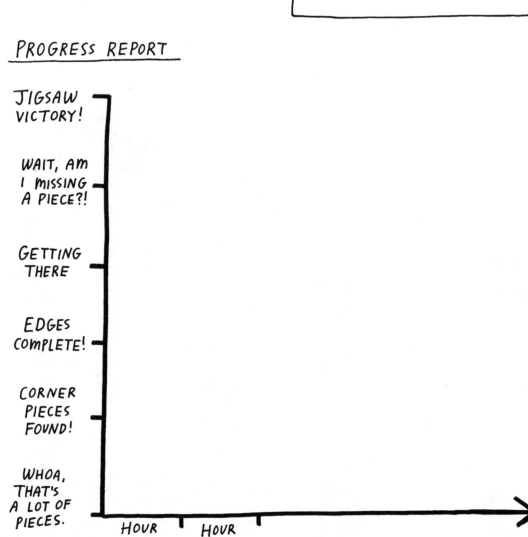

JIGSAW VICTORY!

WAIT, AM I MISSING A PIECE?!

GETTING THERE

EDGES COMPLETE!

CORNER PIECES FOUND!

WHOA, THAT'S A LOT OF PIECES.

HOUR ONE        HOUR TWO

# FIND YOUR OWN HIDEAWAY

Keep your eyes peeled for a place you can escape to whenever you need some time to yourself, away from everyday life. Somewhere to sit, collect your thoughts, maybe read a book. It could be a tucked-away park bench, a shady tree to lie under, or the quietest corner of your local library. Go for a walk! See what you can find.

OPTION A

OPTION B

PRO:

PRO:

CON:

CON:

# HAVE A GOOD CRY TOGETHER

Invite a friend or loved one to join you in this experiment, maybe someone you don't often (or ever) get too emotional with. Look online for three classic or surprising tear-jerker movies. Pick ones that neither of you have seen before and host a movie marathon! Or a few movie nights together. Make yourselves some popcorn and, of course, keep the tissues handy.

WE BOTH AGREE THAT THIS MOVIE NIGHT IS A SAFE SPACE—MEANING IF THE WATER WORKS FLOW, WE LET THEM FLOW! 000

signed: _____ & _____

| FIRST MOVIE: | ☐ DRY EYES | ☐ DRY EYES |
|---|---|---|
| | ☐ SINGLE TEAR | ☐ SINGLE TEAR |
| | ☐ WATERWORKS | ☐ WATERWORKS |
| SECOND MOVIE: | ☐ DRY EYES | ☐ DRY EYES |
| | ☐ SINGLE TEAR | ☐ SINGLE TEAR |
| | ☐ WATERWORKS | ☐ WATERWORKS |
| THIRD MOVIE: | ☐ DRY EYES | ☐ DRY EYES |
| | ☐ SINGLE TEAR | ☐ SINGLE TEAR |
| | ☐ WATERWORKS | ☐ WATERWORKS |

# BUY A STRANGE-LOOKING FOOD AT THE SUPERMARKET

## HOW TO PREPARE & EAT IT

(Look it up online when you get home.)

## WHAT'S YOUR VERDICT?

☐ TASTE SENSATION!

☐ It was . . . interesting.

☐ Just, no.

☐ All of the above

43

# LET LUCK DECIDE HOW YOU MOVE YOUR BODY

1) Clear a dance floor at home.
2) Put on your most feel-good album or playlist.
3) Flip a coin to begin!

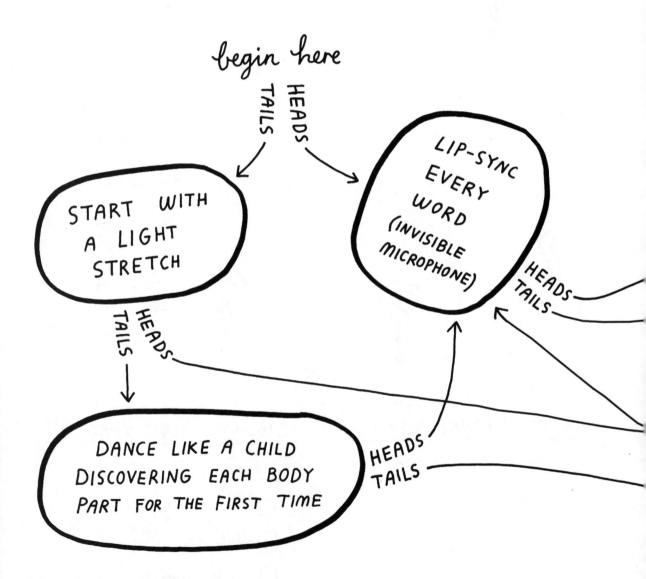

begin here

TAILS • HEADS

START WITH A LIGHT STRETCH

LIP-SYNC EVERY WORD (INVISIBLE MICROPHONE)

HEADS • TAILS

TAILS • HEADS

DANCE LIKE A CHILD DISCOVERING EACH BODY PART FOR THE FIRST TIME

HEADS • TAILS

# TINY BUCKET LIST
### (PART ONE)

☐ TO TAKE MY FIRST BITE OF _____

☐ TO HAVE A COFFEE WITH THIS INTERNET FRIEND:

☐ TO LISTEN TO THIS ALBUM IN FULL:

☐ _____

☐ _____

☐ _____

Think about some of the more bite-size & inexpensive adventures to put on your bucket list: new experiences that you can have in a day, or even an hour!

# PEEL & EAT A CLEMENTINE
## IN THE SUNSHINE
### VERY SLOWLY

DRIPS OF JUICE
HERE FOR PROOF

# BEGIN A COLLECTION

- [ ] NOVELTY COFFEE MUGS
- [ ] OTHER PEOPLE'S SHOPPING LISTS
- [ ] CACTUS PLANTS
- [ ] _____

the very first item in my
new collection!

# COMPLIMENT A STRANGER

Try to notice something other than how they look... a kind thing you see them do, how nice their vibe is, or a skill you appreciate them sharing with the world. Give your compliments in person, rather than online.

## THREE COMPLIMENTS I GAVE THIS WEEK
(and who I gave them to):

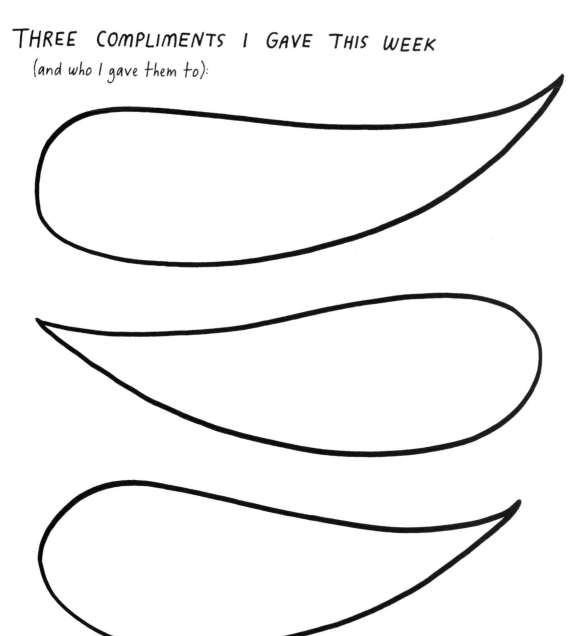

# FEEL SOMETHING OTHER THAN PRETTY

Save this activity for a day when you look in the mirror & don't feel so happy with what you see. Maybe it's a new crop of stress pimples, your hair won't do what you want it to do, or you're just in a funky mood. It's fine to feel this way sometimes!

We get beaten down with so many messages every day telling us that we must look gorgeous & flawless at all times. On social media we follow celebrities with their own personal makeup artists, and hundreds of companies every day try to sell us happiness & self-worth in a tub of moisturizer or a new mascara.

Today you looked in the mirror and didn't feel so pretty. That's okay. Choose to feel something else instead.

### Here are some ideas
(choose a favorite for today):

I FEEL... PLAYFUL, STRONG, POWERFUL, SPORTY, ADVENTUROUS, REBELLIOUS, FRIENDLY, BRAVE, PASSIONATE, CREATIVE, WELL-READ, OBSERVANT, CURIOUS, PREPARED, IN LOVE, FESTIVE, FUNNY...

or add a few of your own!

# TODAY I FEEL _____.

In what ways can you act out this feeling today?

WHAT YOU WEAR:

WHO YOU CHOOSE TO
SPEND TIME WITH:

WHAT YOU AVOID:

WHAT YOU SEEK OUT:

WHERE YOU GO:

HOW YOU CARRY
YOURSELF:

# MAKE A MUSIC VIDEO
## FOR SOMEONE

It could be as simple as recording the video on your phone in one take. Gather some friends or family to lip-sync & dance with you—or fly solo!

PERSON WHO I THINK DESERVES SOME LOVE:

this is for _____ ♡

A SONG THAT'D MAKE THEM SMILE!

SCOUT A LOCATION:
in the backyard? at the park?

HOW ABOUT PROPS? COSTUME IDEAS?
WHO'S THE CHOREOGRAPHER?

# GO ON A
# MIDNIGHT MISSION

Brainstorm a few places you've never visited at 12:00 a.m. when most of the town is sleeping. Things to do that might feel extra special or exciting in the moonlight:

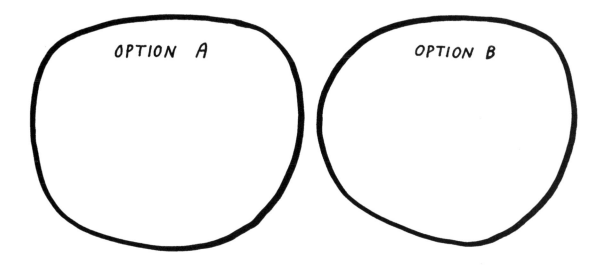

OPTION A

OPTION B

BRING A FRIEND?

THE MISSION, SHOULD WE CHOOSE TO ACCEPT...

A few ideas: Play a board game in the park with a flashlight, park your car near the airport to watch the midnight planes land overhead, or take a cool dip in your friend's pool under the stars!

# DISCOVER A NEW OUTFIT
## IN YOUR WARDROBE

mix & match what you already have in new ways. Throw together items that you really don't think will work. Dig deep in the back for accessories you'd forgotten about. Put on some music that will get you in a playful mood.

Sketch here the most interesting outfits you come up with!

Also note: How do these outfits make you feel? Do they remind you of something? If they give you a personality shift (or even a secret identity), describe it.

TRY THESE:

☐ monochrome from head to toe   ☐ pattern clash   ☐ tuck it in!

☐ something really casual with something really fancy   ☐ lots of layering

# WATCH THE CLOUDS ROLL BY

Find a grassy patch to lay down on, with a nice view of the sky. Put your phone away. Let your eyes drift along with the clouds. What shapes & faces do you see in the cloud formations? Appreciate them for a moment before they disappear forever. Record some of your favorites here.

# DECIDE ON A NEW WAY TO GREET EACH OTHER

YOU:            YOUR FRIEND:

Here are some options. Discuss & choose one—or add your own!

☐ CLASSIC KISS-ON-CHEEK-&-HUG COMBO

☐ FIST BUMP: CASUAL OR WITH EXPLOSION SOUND
                                    EFFECTS

☐ QUICK EMBRACE

☐ WARM EMBRACE

☐ BEAR HUG!

☐ ELABORATE SECRET HANDSHAKE (to be rehearsed)

☐ ESKIMO KISS

☐ HIGH FIVE!

☐ THE LIFT FROM DIRTY DANCING
    * if there's space for a proper run up

☐ OTHER:

DO YOU BOTH AGREE?

SIGNED: _____ & _____

# ATTEND A PEACEFUL PROTEST

WHEN:                  WHERE:

Who or what are you showing up in support of? Why is this important to you?

Design a sign to take with you!

# HAVE A STRANGER
# PLAN YOUR DAY

Ask someone you don't know very well (or at all) to suggest three ways you could spend your day in your current city/town. Ask them, what are their favorite places to visit? what are their favorite things to do? Let them know your budget & how much time you have. See what they come up with for you!

FIRST DO THIS:

THEN THIS:

& IF YOU HAVE TIME:

# INTERVIEW SOMEONE WHO'S NOT ON SOCIAL MEDIA

NAME:                                    NICKNAME:

WHAT DO YOU WANT MORE OF THIS YEAR?

## MORE

WHAT DO YOU WANT LESS OF?

## LESS

IF YOU HAD TO DESCRIBE YOURSELF IN THREE IMAGES, WHAT WOULD THEY BE?

IN THE STORY OF YOUR LIFE, WHAT WOULD THE CHAPTER YOU'RE CURRENTLY LIVING BE CALLED?

# INTERVIEW SOMEONE WITH RED HAIR

NAME: _____     NICKNAME: _____

WHAT DO YOU WANT MORE OF THIS YEAR?

## MORE

WHAT DO YOU WANT LESS OF?

## LESS

IF YOU HAD TO DESCRIBE YOURSELF IN THREE IMAGES, WHAT WOULD THEY BE?

 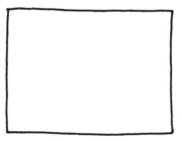 

IN THE STORY OF YOUR LIFE, WHAT WOULD THE CHAPTER YOU'RE CURRENTLY LIVING BE CALLED?

# INTERVIEW SOMEONE WHO WAS BORN IN ANOTHER COUNTRY

NAME:                           NICKNAME:

WHAT DO YOU WANT MORE OF THIS YEAR?

# MORE

WHAT DO YOU WANT LESS OF?

# LESS

IF YOU HAD TO DESCRIBE YOURSELF IN THREE IMAGES,
WHAT WOULD THEY BE?

IN THE STORY OF YOUR LIFE, WHAT WOULD THE
CHAPTER YOU'RE CURRENTLY LIVING BE CALLED?

# INTERVIEW YOUR DAD

## (OR SOMEONE ELSE'S DAD)

NAME:                          NICKNAME:

WHAT DO YOU WANT MORE OF THIS YEAR?

# MORE

WHAT DO YOU WANT LESS OF?

# LESS

IF YOU HAD TO DESCRIBE YOURSELF IN THREE IMAGES, WHAT WOULD THEY BE?

 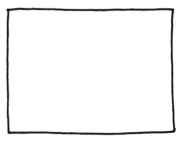 

IN THE STORY OF YOUR LIFE, WHAT WOULD THE CHAPTER YOU'RE CURRENTLY LIVING BE CALLED?

# HOST A CRAFTERNOON

WHEN:                          WHERE: (your house?)

WHO MIGHT BE KEEN TO JOIN:

☐

☐

☐

CRAFT SUPPLIES WE CAN PLAY WITH:

BEVERAGES WE CAN SIP:          SNACKS WE CAN
                                SNACK ON:

# SEND AN OVERDUE APOLOGY TO SOMEONE

sorry
for

How I will try to make it up to you:

SORRY

# WRITE A SHORT STORY
## IN 12 HOURS

① Set a timer on your phone to go off every hour from 9:00 a.m. to 9:00 p.m.

② When the alarm rings, pause whatever you're doing & add a quick sentence to your story. Try to include at least one of these words (or all four)—"goldfish," "ginger," "ice cream truck," and "hopeful."

③ Repeat for 12 hours & add the final sentence at 9:00 p.m. Read the whole thing to yourself (or whoever else might be with you) in bed tonight!

| | |
|---|---|
| 9:00 a.m. | |
| 10:00 a.m. | |
| 11:00 a.m. | |
| 12:00 p.m. | |
| 1:00 p.m. | |
| 2:00 p.m. | |

3:00 p.m.

4:00 p.m.

5:00 p.m.

6:00 p.m.

7:00 p.m.

8:00 p.m.

9:00 p.m.

# GET CREATIVE WITH YOUR SMALL TALK

Instead of the usual "So, what do you do?," what else could you ask someone you're meeting for the first time? Brainstorm some open-ended questions that might spark a more meaningful or playful conversation.

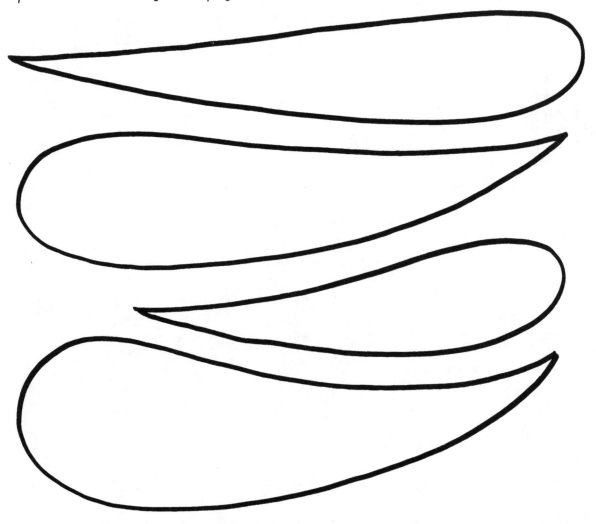

Try them out in social situations this week! Don't be disheartened if they flop . . . that person might have other things on their mind. Try again with someone else!

# INVENT A NEW RECIPE
# FOR DINNER TONIGHT

I CALL THIS DISH:

THE SPECIAL INGREDIENT IS:

IS IT GOING ON THE WEEKLY MENU?

☐ Yes! Perfect as is!   ☐ Needs a few tweaks.   ☐ Let's not speak of this again.

# LET A DOG TAKE you FOR A WALK

*your own pup or a friend's dog!

A MAP OF OUR WALK (drawn from memory)

Let go of any ambitions about where you should be headed or how quick your pace should be. Zigzag, strut, pause, wander off the sidewalk. Whatever your dog guide stops to look at, you look at, too.

mark some of the stops you made along the way. What you saw, smelled, and heard!

# ASK A CHILD
# FOR ADVICE

Think of some personal questions using the prompts below. Is there a young one in your family you could ask? Perhaps a friend's child? Listen thoughtfully for any nuggets of youthful wisdom they might share with you.

✳ I DON'T LIKE MY _____. WHAT SHOULD I DO ABOUT THAT?

✳ HOW DO I KNOW WHEN I'M READY TO _____ _____?

✳ A RELATIONSHIP OR DATING QUESTION: _____ _____

✳ I'M FEELING _____! IF YOU WERE ME, WHAT WOULD YOU DO?

# PICK YOURSELF SOME FLOWERS

Go hunting for wildflowers at the park. Maybe sweet-talk your neighbor with the blooming garden. Put your little bouquet in a glass of water next to your bed or on your desk, somewhere just for you.

# GET TO KNOW
# A WORKMATE BETTER

## (OR CLASSMATE)

Who is someone you often see at work
or school, but don't know very well?

### THREE THINGS I'VE NOTICED ABOUT THEM:

Think of some questions to ask them this week, more interesting than the usual
small talk. What are you curious to learn?

☐ WHAT WERE YOU LIKE AS A CHILD?

☐ _____

☐ _____

☐ _____

# DIY FILM SCHOOL

Cut out this poster to stick on your fridge at home, or above your desk at work. Ask any visitors or workmates to jot down their all-time favorite movies for you. Maybe you'll have seen some already, but be prepared to expand your cinematic horizons! Consider this list your remedy for any movie night indecision. Also, so satisfying to tick them off one by one.

- - - - - - - - - - - - - - - - - - - - - - - - - - - - - - -

# MOVIES YOU LOVE?

ALL-TIME FAVORITES!  ANY GENRE!  DOCUMENTARIES, TOO, PLEASE!

☐ _____     ☐ _____
☐ _____     ☐ _____
☐ _____     ☐ _____
☐ _____     ☐ _____
☐ _____     ☐ _____
☐ _____     ☐ _____
☐ _____     ☐ _____
☐ _____     ☐ _____
☐ _____     ☐ _____
☐ _____     ☐ _____
☐ _____     ☐ _____
☐ _____     ☐ _____

# PLAN (& MAKE)
# A PICNIC FOR ONE

Pack your favorite snacks, beverage, book to read, blanket to lie on, hat to nap under. Enjoy the fresh air & your own company for a few hours!

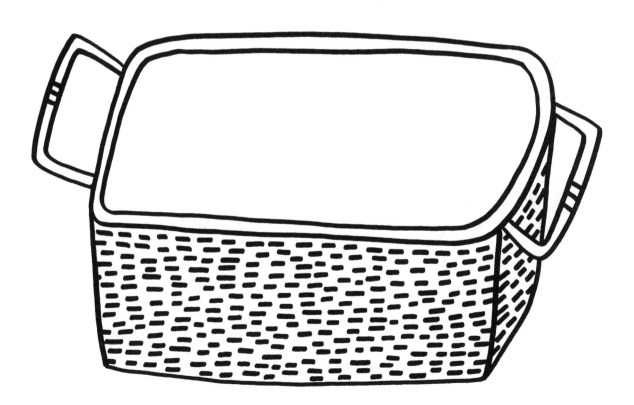

A PRETTY PLACE TO PICNIC:

# BE AN OPTIMIST FOR THE DAY

Fill out this page soon after waking up in the morning. Take a quiet moment with your cup of tea or coffee to practice some gratitude. In the sunshine, if you can!

## THREE THINGS I'M THANKFUL FOR IN MY LIFE:

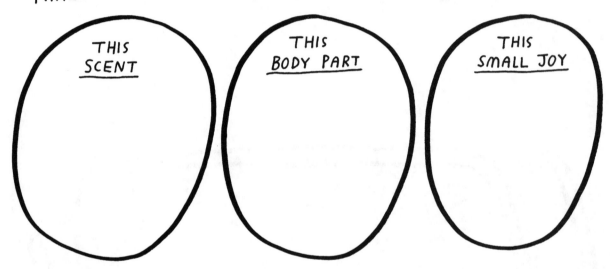

THIS SCENT

THIS BODY PART

THIS SMALL JOY

## SOMETHING TO BE EXCITED ABOUT TODAY:

Fill out this page in the evening before you go to bed. Take a quiet moment to reflect on your day and focus on the good things in your life.

A BEAUTIFUL THING
I SAW TODAY:

A SMALL VICTORY!

THREE THINGS I'm THANKFUL FOR IN MY LIFE:

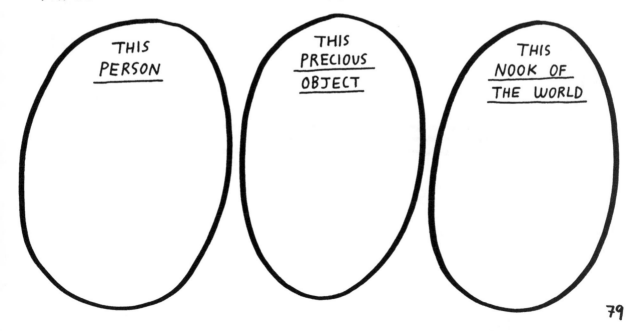

THIS
PERSON

THIS
PRECIOUS
OBJECT

THIS
NOOK OF
THE WORLD

# REVISIT A PLACE FROM YOUR CHILDHOOD

Before you go, draw everything you remember about it.

After you visit . . . what's changed? What's stayed the same?

# RIP OFF THE BAND-AID!

What are some small tasks (half hour or less) that you've been avoiding lately? The ones you keep pushing farther down your to-do list. Jot down three things that come to mind. It might be a phone call, a house chore, a work thing.

Do one of those tasks right now, and enjoy that sweet relief afterward!

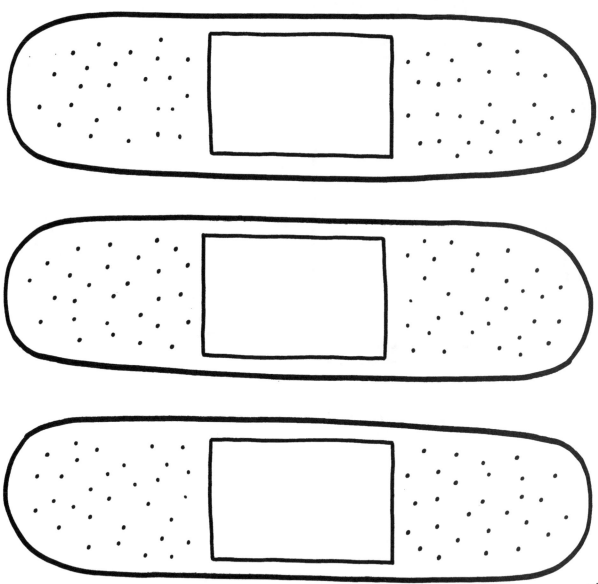

# GO ON A SILENT DATE

Ask a friend (or someone you fancy!) to meet you for dinner this week. All evening, agree to give each other the friendliest kind of silent treatment. Communicate only through doodling! Bring along this page, some pens, and a little sketchbook for writing more notes to each other throughout your meal.

## DOODLE A PORTRAIT OF EACH OTHER:

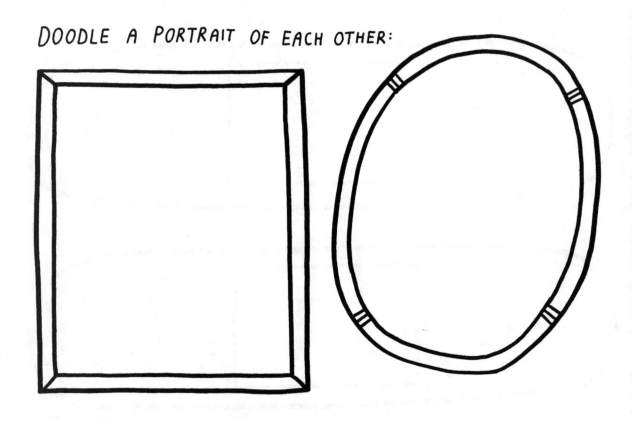

## TWO TRUTHS & A LIE! (GUESS WHICH IS THE LIE)

1.

2.

3.

STARING CONTEST?

WINNER GETS TO:
LOSER HAS TO:

DESIGN A TATTOO
FOR EACH OTHER.
POINT TO WHERE
THEY SHOULD GET IT.

MAKE UP A STORY TOGETHER,
ONE LINE AT A TIME...

Once upon a time

# SHOW UP TO AN EVENT
# YOU'RE NERVOUS ABOUT

## you're invited

WHAT:

WHERE:

WHEN:

WHO MIGHT BE THERE:

RSVP—

☐ YES, I'LL SHOW UP FOR AT LEAST ___ MINUTES
& TRY TO _____

# ORGANIZE A
# TREASURE HUNT

FIRST CLUE

SECOND CLUE

THIRD CLUE

What will the treasure be?

Who are you organizing the treasure hunt for?

# WRITE YOUR AUTOBIOGRAPHY
## WITH MUSIC

Try to tell your life story (so far) in 12 songs! Start with your childhood, family, teenage years, significant loves, life-changing moments . . . all the way to now.

♫ PLAYLIST TITLE:

1.

2.

3.

4.

5.

6.

7.

8.

9.

10.

11.

12.

# SWAP COMPLIMENTS WITH A FRIEND

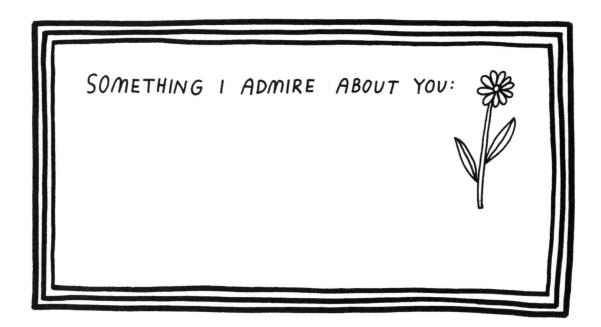

SOMETHING I ADMIRE ABOUT YOU:

SOMETHING YOU ADMIRE ABOUT ME:

# NOTICE THE TINY DETAILS
# OF A PERSON's FACE

**CHOSEN PERSON:**

(someone you'll be seeing this week)

While you're together try to notice the exact colors of their eyes, the length of their eyelashes, the soft hairs on their cheeks and upper lip, that stray freckle on their collarbone, the tiny crinkles near their mouth when they smile.

When you think you've noticed it all, take another look! Find something else!

## SKETCHES & NOTES

(drawn from memory)

# THE COLOR OF THE DAY
## IS BLUE

As you go about your business today allow yourself to notice the color BLUE everywhere. Choose something BLUE when you get dressed today. Be attracted to the color BLUE in what you buy, which shops you walk into, the books you pick up, what you eat for lunch, and who you smile at on the sidewalk.

### MY PERSONAL INVENTORY
### OF blue things*

*Clothing, books, artwork & other BLUE things you own.

Follow the color BLUE today! Where does it lead you?
Map out all the BLUE in your day.

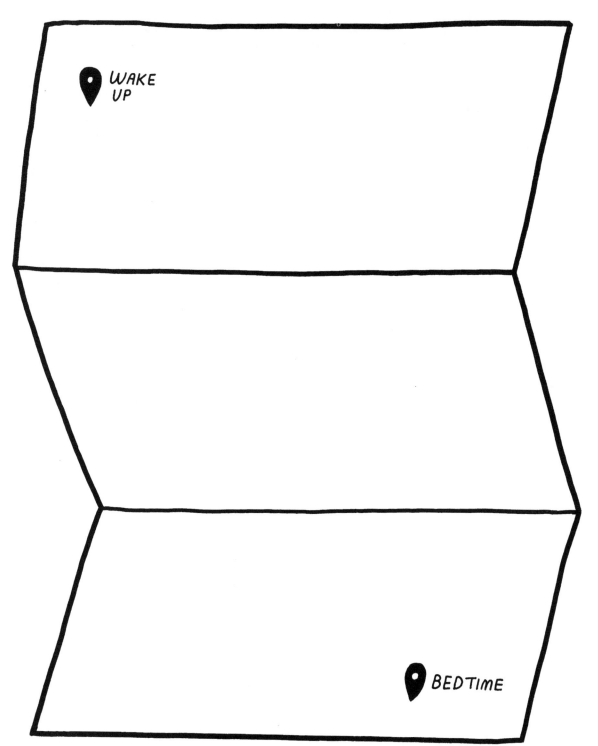

# REDISCOVER A HOBBY
## YOU LOVED AS A KID

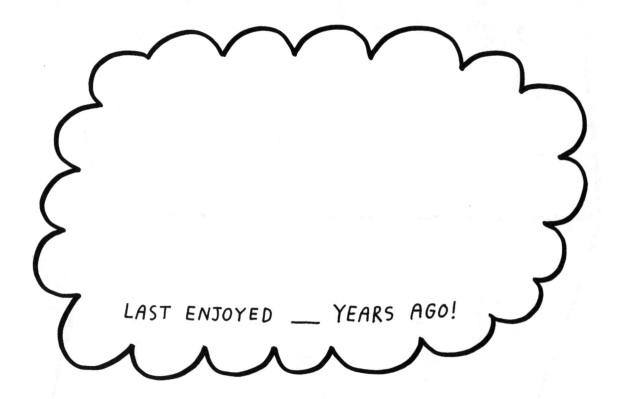

LAST ENJOYED ___ YEARS AGO!

What did you like about it so much?     Equipment/supplies you need to gather:

# FIND A NEW TEAM
## TO CHEER FOR

Search online for a local sporting event that you don't know much (or anything at all) about.

- ☐ BEACH VOLLEYBALL
- ☐ QUIDDITCH
- ☐ NETBALL

- ☐ TENPIN BOWLING
- ☐ ROLLER DERBY
- ☐ _____

Pick a team to support and show up to their next game. Get in the spirit!

_____ VS _____

WHEN:

WHERE:

wear the → team colors

# GUESS THE LYRICS

First, think of a song you mumble along to because you don't know what most of the words are:

Now try to write out all the lyrics below. You can listen to the song, but don't look up any of the lyrics online. Take as many wild guesses as you need to!

NEW & (maybe) IMPROVED *lyrics* BY _____

# HOST A THEMED
## DINNER PARTY

Choose a theme!

☐ (A TV SHOW OR BOOK YOU LOVE?)
☐ CHILDREN'S BIRTHDAY PARTY
☐ STUCK ON AN ISLAND TOGETHER
☐ _____

What we'll eat

What we'll wear

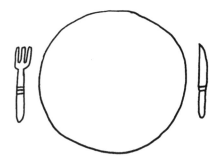

A game to play

The perfect music choice

# TAKE THE "NEXT STEP" IN YOUR FRIENDSHIP

## (or RELATIONSHIP)

This could be with your best friend, or a new crush. Have a think about what the "next step" might be for you as a twosome. It could be a silly thing, a thoughtful thing, something meaningful to you both. It's fun to be cute with your mates.

HERE'S MY WI-FI PASSWORD

I GOT YOU A TOOTHBRUSH FOR MY PLACE

LET'S NOT HOLD OUR FARTS IN ANYMORE! (LET IT RIP)

TO: _____

I APPRECIATE YOU SO MUCH AS A _____ & I THINK IT'S TIME WE TAKE OUR RELATIONSHIP TO THE "NEXT LEVEL"...

xx

WITH LOVE,

Snip out the heart & deliver it to your friend.
You might also include a small gift, something related to the "next step"—such as a framed internet meme, a new toothbrush, or a can of beans! (see: previous page).

# SIGN UP FOR A CLASS YOU'VE ALWAYS WANTED TO TRY

## SO YOU WANT TO TRY _____ ?

WE'VE GOT A CLASS FOR YOU!

WHERE —

WHEN —

WHAT TO BRING —

SEE YOU THERE? (circle one)

I'm nervous,
but . . . SURE!

Yay!!!
Can't wait.

Let's do this!
(finally)

# SAY THE THING YOU'VE BEEN WANTING TO SAY

Think of someone in your life who you're close with. What have you never told them but wish you could say? Maybe you're nervous because you don't know how they'll react, or maybe it's just never felt like the "right moment" (is there ever a perfect moment, though?).

This week, tell them. Be vulnerable! Be brave! Practice what you'll say here.

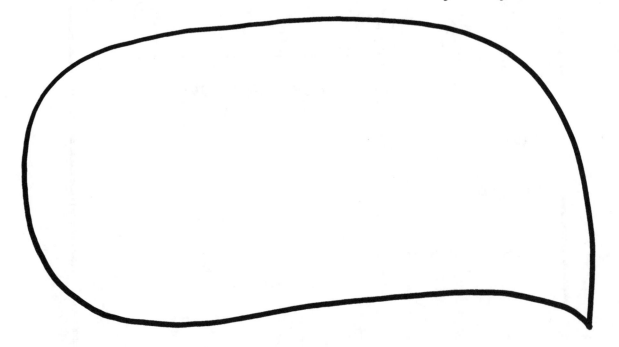

How do you worry they'll respond?          How do you hope they'll respond?

# BE A TOURIST IN
# YOUR OWN CITY/TOWN

First, do a quick search online:

| TOURIST THINGS TO DO IN [YOUR TOWN] | Q |

| UNUSUAL THINGS TO DO IN [YOUR CITY] | Q |

Now make yourself an itinerary for the day:

| 10:00 a.m. | 12:00 p.m. | 2:00 p.m. |
|---|---|---|
|  |  |  |

# PARTAKE IN A BIT OF PEOPLE-WATCHING

Take a seat at a busy café (or on a park bench) with this page open & a pen at the ready. Fill out an imaginary bio for any strangers who catch your eye. No need to stare . . . a quick glance will do! Try to let go of any stereotypes that come up, but let your imagination have some fun.

## STRANGER #1

OBSERVATIONAL
SKETCHES:

THEIR NAME MIGHT BE . . .

I LIKE THE WAY THEY . . .

MAYBE THEY'RE ON THEIR WAY TO . . .

## STRANGER #2

THEIR NAME MIGHT BE...

THEIR MOST PRIZED POSSESSION
MIGHT BE...

MAYBE THEY RUN A PROJECT CALLED...


## STRANGER #3

THEIR NAME MIGHT BE...

THE MOST INTERESTING THING ABOUT
THEM MIGHT BE...

THERE MIGHT BE LEFTOVER _____
IN THEIR FRIDGE BECAUSE...

# KEEP A SPECIAL MOMENT ALL TO YOURSELF

The next time you see something beautiful or interesting or hilarious, & the urge is to get out your phone to take a photo of it or to tell a friend . . . pause instead. Pause & enjoy this small thing. Keep it as a secret between you & the universe.

Write (or draw) about it here, but only in a way no one else would understand.

# CAFÉS & RESTAURANTS
## I'VE YET TO VISIT

☐

☐

☐

☐

☐

☐

Do a search online for interesting places—some nearby and some that give you a chance to explore a new neighborhood. Pick somewhere from the list to visit this week. Bring along a friend & go for a walk around the block after your meal.

# ENJOY AN UNSOLVED MYSTERY

While you're out in the world today, think of a mystery you've yet to solve . . . like, why do humans get the hiccups? Why is there a light in the refrigerator but not the freezer? Where did my lost sock really disappear to?

Ignore the urge to look up any answers online! Instead, mull the question over in your imagination all day & come up with a few theories of your own.

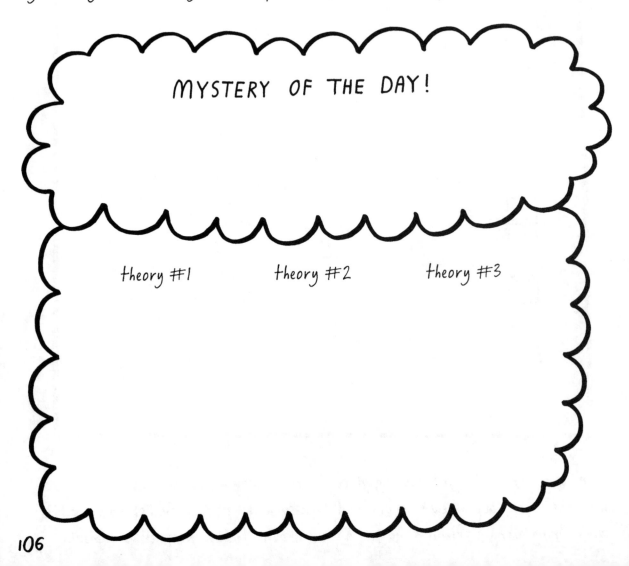

MYSTERY OF THE DAY!

theory #1          theory #2          theory #3

# BE FANCY
# IN YOUR OWN HOME

One normal afternoon, decide to be very fancy for the rest of the evening . . .

SUGGESTIONS: French café music. The film Breakfast At Tiffany's as your muse! Dim the lights. Use that candle you've been saving for a special occasion. Bathe or shower yourself in a slow, pampering way. Spritz your favorite scent. Slip on something that makes you feel decadent and cozy, like a freshly washed robe. Something sparkly on your fingers if you're into that sort of thing! A bowl of fresh berries. A plate of chocolates neatly arranged. Sip a fancy beverage from your nicest glass & kick out that pinky finger, darling!

OTHER SMALL, INEXPENSIVE WAYS TO FEEL *fancy* IN MY OWN HOME:

# START A CLUB & HOST YOUR FIRST MEETING

Start small, with a friend or two and a simple idea! You can invite more people later on if you want to.

## WHAT WILL YOUR CLUB BE CALLED?

## WHEN & WHERE WILL YOU MEET?

EVERY _____

AT _____

## THE FOUNDING MEMBERS

&                    &

# WHAT WILL YOU DO AT YOUR FIRST MEETING?

| Eat this: | Talk about: | Play this: |
| --- | --- | --- |
| | | |

# DO MEMBERS NEED TO BRING ANYTHING?

BYO _____

DESIGN A
CLUB EMBLEM

# PRACTICE BEING MORE SPONTANEOUS

Today you choose to do things a little differently. Not that you plan anything in particular, but a certain curiosity has been awakened in you. Today you listen to your whims rather than ignore them. Today you shush your self-doubt. Today you keep your eyes peeled for the small ways the world is trying to connect with you. At least once today you wander off your usual path . . .

## SPONTANEOUS DOODLING WARM-UP
(Keep going until you run out of space.)

# FINISH READING THAT BOOK

Carve out a few hours in your week to enjoy some reading. Is there a book you've been meaning to finish, or even one you've been hoping to begin?

**READING NOOK OF CHOICE:**
(with a cup of tea? or afternoon beer?)


**FAVORITE SENTENCE SO FAR:**

# GO ON A TWO-PART OUTING
## WITH SOMEONE IN YOUR FAMILY

FIRST, SOMETHING _THEY_ WANT TO DO:

Your thoughts before?

Your thoughts after?

1) Choose things you've never done together before.
2) Agree to both be a good sport about it.
3) You might like to put a limit on it . . . say, one hour each?

## THEN, SOMETHING <u>YOU</u> WANT TO DO:

| | |
|---|---|
| Their thoughts before? | Their thoughts after? |

# LISTEN TO YOUR OWN ADVICE

What's something you've been confused, unsure, or stressed about lately? Vent about it here. Let it all out!

Now pretend a good friend has come to you with the same worry. What advice would you give to them? What comforting words or tough love would you offer your friend?

# GIVE SOMEONE A (TEMPORARY) TATTOO

First find a willing client to tattoo. Now prepare some designs for them to choose from—perhaps ask them a bit about their life, what they love most, and the kind of tattoo they have in mind. Then use a nontoxic marker on the skin!

TATTOO FLASH

# LEARN A NEW WORD

Use a random word generator (look one up online) to find a perfect new word to sprinkle into your conversations. Choose a word you don't yet know the meaning of but it seems fun to say aloud.

WORD OF THE DAY:

DEFINITION:

WHY I LIKE THIS WORD:

HOW TO USE IT IN A SENTENCE TODAY:

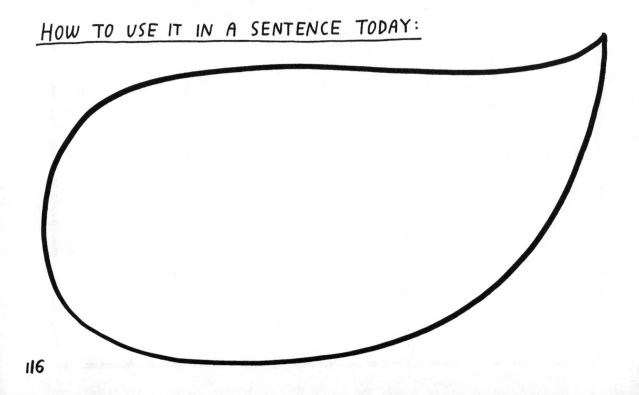

# WRITE A POSITIVE REVIEW FOR A HOME-COOKED MEAL

The next time someone is kind enough to cook you dinner, fill out this five-star review for them, to say thank you!

## DINNER *was* SERVED!

REVIEW BY:

COOKED BY CHEF _____

AT CASA _____

⭐ ⭐ ⭐ ⭐ ⭐  FIVE-STAR MEAL!

MADE WITH LOVE & _____

_____

HIGHLIGHT OF THE EVENING:

_____

_____

_____

WOULD VISIT AGAIN? DUH! / NAH

LEAVE A TIP: _____

_____

# TINY BUCKET LIST

## (PART TWO)

☐ TO VISIT THIS PLACE I ALWAYS WALK PAST BUT NEVER GO IN:

☐ TO SPEND A WHOLE EVENING _____

☐ TO GET UP AN HOUR EARLY TO _____

☐ _____

☐ _____

☐ _____

Think about some of the more bite-size & inexpensive adventures to put on your bucket list: new experiences that you can have in a day, or even an hour!

# CAMP OUT AT HOME

Pitch a tent in your living room or build yourself a blanket fort to spend the night in. There's no Wi-Fi at this campsite, so hide away your devices . . . unless it's to screen a continuous video of a crackling campfire on your laptop (they're easy to find online), that could make for some nice ambience!

## FAVORITE CAMPING FOOD:

☐ FAIRY LIGHTS

☐ THERMOS OF HOT CHOCOLATE

☐ EVERY PILLOW & BLANKET
    YOU CAN FIND

☐ FLASHLIGHT! (LIGHTS OFF)

Who's camping with you?

SOUNDS
of the
RAIN FOREST

# PLAY CUPID

## FOR FRIENDSHIP!

Think of two friends who don't know each other but you suspect they'd get along really well. Introduce them! Invite them out for a drink with you. See if there's any friendship sparks!

# OFFER TO HELP

Keep a few hours free this weekend & give them to someone you care about, to use however they please! Your neighbor might appreciate a babysitter while they run some errands; your grandma might need a little help around the house. Maybe your friend is overwhelmed with a task that you're quite handy at. It's only a few hours of your life—enjoy being of service!

FOR:

## gift certificate

_____ HOURS OF MY TIME, WHATEVER YOU NEED! I'M ALL YOURS.

VALID: this weekend any time between

_____ and _____

WITH LOVE, _____

\* Take a photo of the gift certificate & message it to them!

# START AN ANNUAL
# TOURNAMENT

Suggestions: mini golf, basketball shoot-out, charades, or a family board game!

## WHO'S INVITED?
(friends? family? workmates?)

welcome to our 1ST ANNUAL

## BONUS TRADITIONS:
(that may or may not stick)

＊ Everyone is expected to wear

_____

_____

＊ At some random point in the

tournament _____

_____

_____

THE REIGNING CHAMPION!

What prize does the winner receive?

# GO ON A BUG SAFARI

Visit the local park or explore your backyard if you have one. Get down close to the ground, peek into the grass, carefully examine a tree trunk. Keep your eyes peeled for a delicate, camouflaged caterpillar snacking on mint leaves . . . or tiny determined ants carrying home a feast. Just be a quiet observer for a while.

When you find a bug that seems particularly curious, make a note of it here in as much detail as you can. Later, look it up online. Find out everything you can about this interesting little critter.

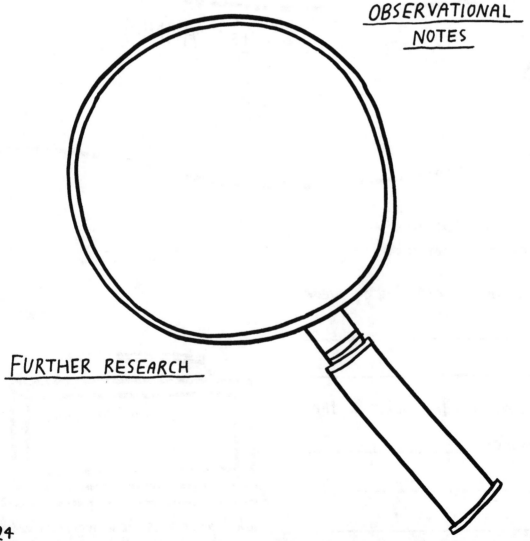

OBSERVATIONAL
NOTES

FURTHER RESEARCH

# ORGANIZE YOUR WARDROBE
## IN ORDER OF COLOR

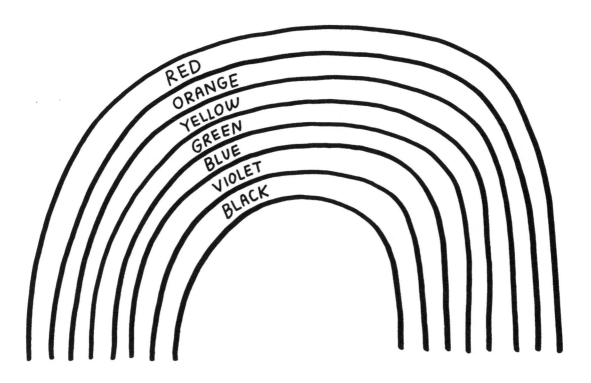

RED
ORANGE
YELLOW
GREEN
BLUE
VIOLET
BLACK

I found so much
of this color:

& hardly any of
this color:

# MAKE A NEW FRIEND

A FRIEND OF MY FRIEND I'VE YET TO MEET
(BUT WOULD LIKE TO!)

WHO THEY ARE:

WHAT WE SEEM TO HAVE
IN COMMON:

GOOD THINGS I'VE HEARD ABOUT THEM:

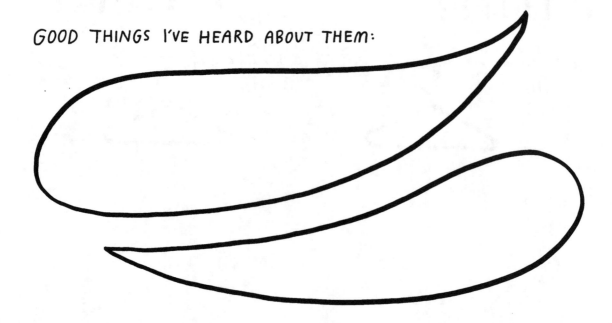

Ask your friend to introduce you, or all go out for a drink together!

# HIDE SILLY NOTES FOR YOUR FUTURE SELF

Use the prompts below to write/doodle some notes that make you smile, or laugh! Now hide them around your house in places you'll likely forget about them for months, even years. You might use tape to stick one behind a photo frame hanging on your wall, bury one in the back of your pantry, or tuck one into an old book.

BADLY DRAWN SELF-PORTRAITS

A LOVE SPELL FOR

_____
(CELEBRITY)

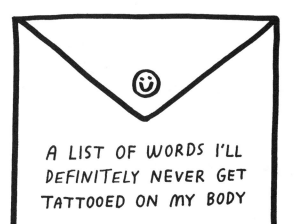

A LIST OF WORDS I'LL DEFINITELY NEVER GET TATTOOED ON MY BODY

UNREALISTIC WISHES FOR MY FUTURE

# SIT WITH AN UNCOMFORTABLE FEELING

Use this page at a time when you need it.

I FEEL... (circle one)

- LONELY  • EMBARRASSED  • UNWORTHY  • LOST

- OTHER:

I WANT TO DISTRACT MYSELF WITH:

BUT INSTEAD I'LL SIT HERE FOR A MOMENT
& TAKE THREE DEEP BREATHS...

one                     two                     three

WHERE IN YOUR BODY IS THIS UNCOMFORTABLE FEELING?
(THROAT? BELLY? CHEST?)

TRY TO DESCRIBE THE PHYSICAL SENSATIONS...
(TINGLING, WARM FACE, HEAVY CHEST, ETC.)

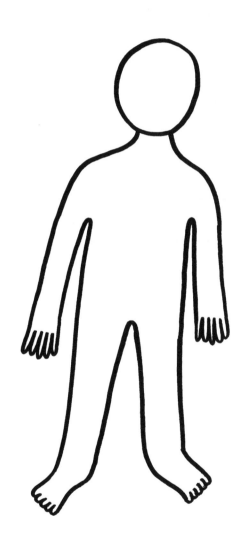

TAKE ANOTHER THREE DEEP BREATHS...

one                    two                    three

# WRITE A SONG

☐ '90s pop song     ☐ country ballad     ☐ children's lullaby

☐ classic rock anthem     ☐ dance floor banger     ☐ _____


VERSE ONE   *Write some lyrics!

YESTERDAY I WENT _____

_____ WAS SO GOOD,

I DIDN'T _____

BUT I PROBABLY SHOULD...

OOOHHH - OOHH!


VERSE TWO


130

# ROMANCE YOURSELF

Whisper something sweet to yourself.

Light some candles.

Give yourself a foot (or hand) massage!

Bring yourself home a little treat.

# DO IT ANYWAY

Think of a plan you recently made and were excited about, but then something got in the way (an unexpected rainstorm, not enough money, not enough time, getting sick . . .) so it never happened. Find a way to do it anyway, this week!

Be okay with a little compromise. Relish the chance to be resourceful & creative! Maybe your favorite band was in town but you couldn't make it to the concert, so you host a themed listening party at your house instead. You invite all your friends who love the band, too, clear a dance floor, & play your favorite album on repeat the whole night. Have some fun conjuring up a plan B!

~~PLAN A~~

PLAN B!

# LEARN A FEW WORDS OF A NEW LANGUAGE

Who do you know who's bilingual? Ask them to teach you!

☐ HINDI   ☐ FRENCH   ☐ JAPANESE

☐ SIGN LANGUAGE   ☐ SPANISH   ☐ _____

HOW TO SAY "HELLO"

TEACH ME A FUNNY SENTENCE.

A FUN
CURSE WORD
TO SAY WHEN
I STUB MY TOE

133

# INTERVIEW THE OLDEST WOMAN YOU KNOW

Record the conversation on your phone, too, so you don't miss anything!

NAME:                                             AGE:

CAN YOU TELL ME ABOUT YOUR FIRST LOVE? HOW DID YOU MEET & WHAT WAS YOUR EARLY RELATIONSHIP LIKE?

IN WHAT WAYS WERE WOMEN TREATED DIFFERENTLY WHEN YOU WERE IN YOUR 20s COMPARED TO NOW?

WHAT ARE SOME MAJOR HISTORICAL EVENTS THAT YOU'VE
LIVED THROUGH (the war, space travel, suffrage, inventions...)
& WHAT DID THEY MEAN TO YOU PERSONALLY?

LOOKING BACK ON YOUR LIFE, WHAT DO YOU WISH YOU'D
DONE DIFFERENTLY?

& WHAT ARE YOU MOST PROUD OF?

135

# PUT UP AN ENCOURAGING POSTER IN YOUR NEIGHBORHOOD

(OR WORKPLACE)

Cut out the poster on the opposite page, cutting along all the dotted lines so that the ribbons hang freely, ready to be plucked! As anonymously as you can (it's more fun that way), stick the poster on a lamppost in your neighborhood using a bit of tape, or pin it on the bulletin board at work. Check back soon to see if any of the ribbons have been claimed!

If you really enjoy the thrill of public art, you can photocopy the page first & stick up a bunch of them all around town.

# ON YOUR MARKS, GET SET, GO!!

1ST
2ND
3RD
4TH
WELL DONE
NICE TRY

# TINY BUCKET LIST
## (PART THREE)

☐ TO *finally* VISIT _____

☐ TO ORGANIZE A NIGHT OF _____

☐ TO LEARN HOW TO _____

☐ _____

☐ _____

☐ _____

Think about some of the more bite-size & inexpensive adventures to put on your bucket list: new experiences that you can have in a day, or even an hour!

# THE COLOR OF THE DAY IS GREEN

As you go about your business today allow yourself to notice the color GREEN everywhere. Choose something GREEN when you get dressed today. Be attracted to the color GREEN in what you buy, which shops you walk into, the books you pick up, what you eat for lunch, and who you smile at on the sidewalk.

## MY PERSONAL INVENTORY
### of green things *

*Clothing, books, artwork, & other GREEN things you own.

Follow the color GREEN today! Where does it lead you?
Map out all the GREEN in your day.

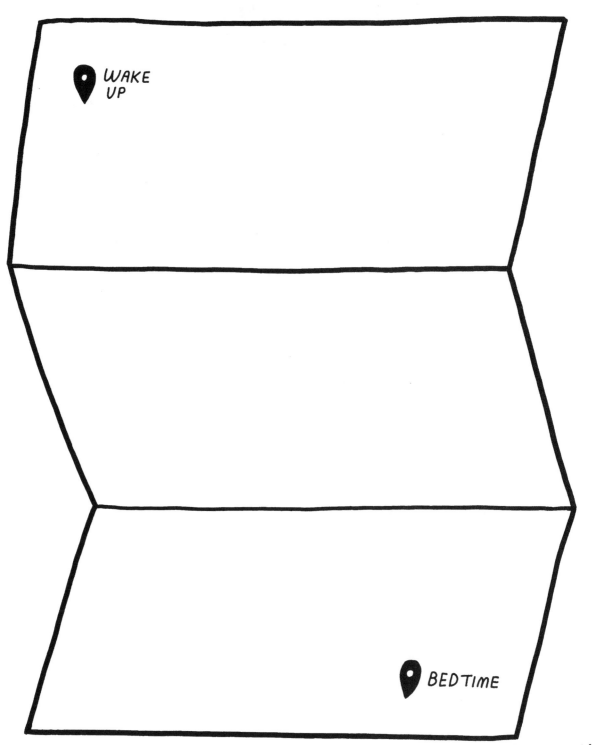

# INVITE YOUR IMAGINATION OUT TO PLAY

Resting in the spine of this page is an invisible ball. Right now it's about the size of a pea, although sometimes it's much bigger. Pick up the tiny ball in your fingers. See, it's got a bit of weight to it? Now throw it in the air and catch it in the palm of your hand . . . now it's an invisible tennis ball! Bounce it on the ground a few times. Has the size changed again? A basketball now, you say? It can be an invisible soccer ball to kick around, too . . . or a big soft beach ball that needs to be thrown awkwardly with both arms out wide!

Your mission for the week is to carry this invisible ball around in your pocket at all times and (when you find a good moment) to play catch with someone. A friend! A stranger on the dance floor! You don't need to explain anything to them, just begin bouncing the invisible ball around and see if they'll catch it. No need to tell them that this invisible ball changes size, they'll figure it out.

If there's room in your pocket, bring along an invisible tennis racket at well.

## DEBRIEF!

WHO DID YOU PLAY CATCH WITH?

HOW DID IT FEEL?

IN WHAT WAYS DID THE BALL MORPH &
CHANGE SHAPE AS YOU PLAYED WITH IT?

# ZOOM IN!

Every day this week take a few photos of your home, your loved ones, the places you go, the things you do . . . but ZOOM IN! Photograph a tiny detail rather than the whole scene. Get as close as you can without the photo being blurry.

At the end of the week, see if you can decipher where all the photos were taken and what they were of. Otherwise, take a wild guess!

WRITE ABOUT A FEW OF THEM HERE:

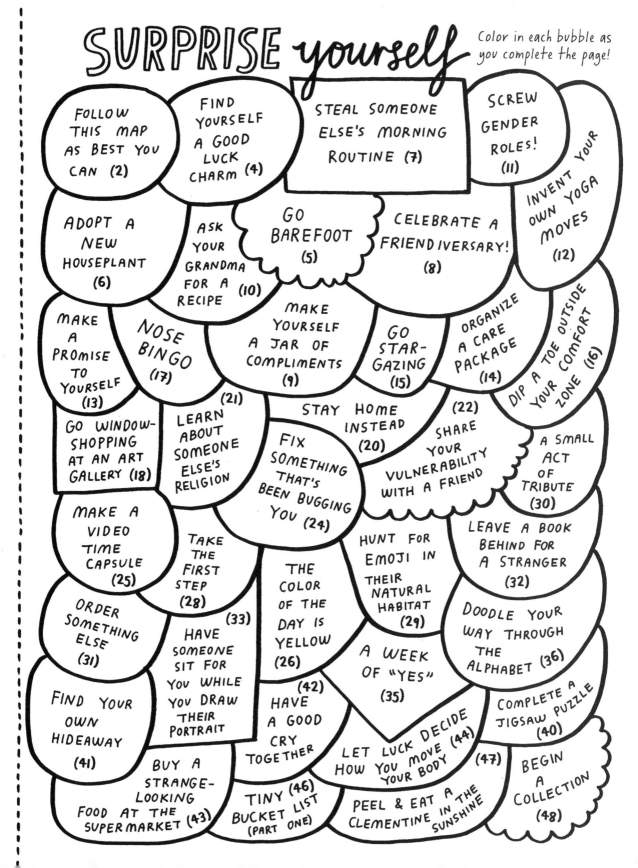

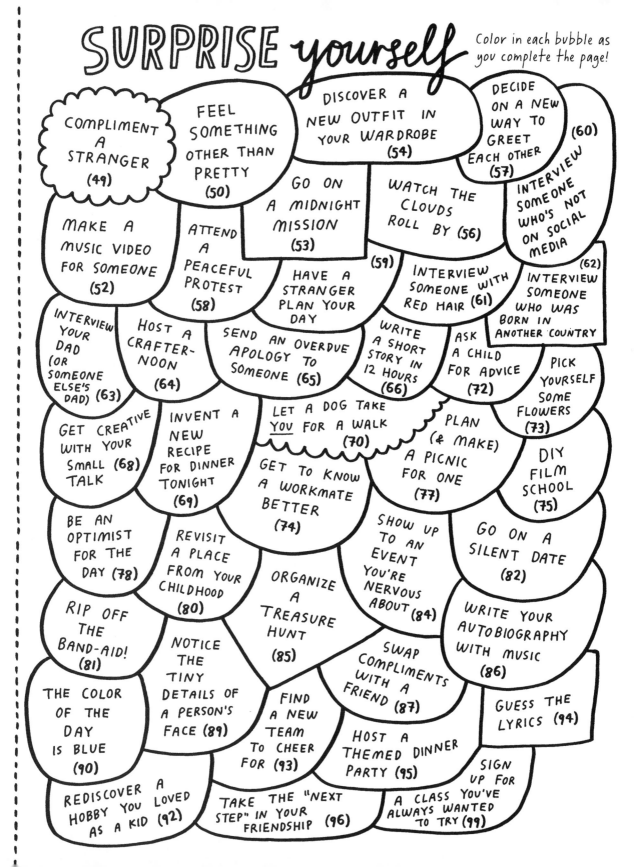

## about the author

Lisa Currie is the author of The Positivity Kit, Me, You, Us, & The Scribble Diary. She lives & plays in Melbourne, Australia. A few things she's fond of are plants, dancing in her kitchen, and hanging out with other people's dogs.

Visit her online: www.lisacurrie.com
Send snail mail: PO BOX 200, Carlton North 3054, Victoria, Australia.

## THANK YOU! ♡

To Sorche—for sending me ideas that sparked many more, & for the pep talk you gave me in the scramble to finish this book. I feel lucky to have you on my team.

To Marian & the folks at TarcherPerigee—as always, I'm chuffed to be able to work with you. It's an actual dream come true! I'm thankful (and smug) that my publisher is so NICE.

To my mum—what would I do without you? You're always only a phone call away. I'm so glad you recently learned how to send animated GIFs of celebratory fireworks and encouraging slogans. Love you lots!

# OTHER BOOKS by LISA CURRIE

Available at all good bookstores!

## the positivity kit

A creative space for you to draw, write, doodle over, and cut & paste. Soon it'll be a handmade map that can guide you back to your happiest self, back to your sweet spot in life. Whenever you need it.

## me, you, us

A book to fill out together with your friends or a loved one. Write fortune cookies to each other! Decide on your perfect theme song! Brainstorm ideas for your matching tattoos!

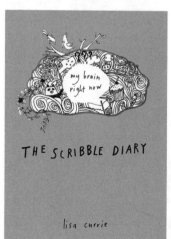

## the scribble diary

Welcome to your own playful, personal doodling space—to vent your thoughts, reflect on your day, and jot down what's in your brain right now.